Science Experiments

Experiments
You Can Do
in Your Kitchen

WATERBIRD BOOKS

Columbus, Ohio

President: Vincent F. Douglas

Publisher: Tracey E. Dils

Project Editors: Joanna Callihan and Nathan Hemmelgarn

Contributors: Q.L. Pearce, Barbara Saffer, Ph.D., Sophie Sheppard,

Leo Abbett, and Neal Yamamoto

Art Directors: Robert Sanford and Christopher Fowler

Interior Design and Production: Jennifer Bowers

Cover Design: Jennifer Bowers

This product has been aligned to state and national organization standards using the Align to Achieve Standards Database. Align to Achieve, Inc., is an independent, not-for-profit organization that facilitates the evaluation and improvement of academic standards and student achievement. To find how this product aligns to your standards, go to www.MHstandards.com.

 **Children's Publishing**

This edition published in the United States of America in 2003 by Waterbird Books,
an imprint of McGraw-Hill Children's Publishing,
a Division of The McGraw-Hill Companies
8787 Orion Place
Columbus, Ohio 43240-4027

www.MHkids.com

Library of Congress Cataloging-in-Publication Data is on file with the publisher.

Printed in the United States of America.

1-57768-623-3

1 2 3 4 5 6 7 8 9 10 PHXBK 09 08 07 06 05 04 03

Experiments You Can Do in Your Kitchen

Contents

- Getting Started in the Kitchen — 4
- Lights Out — 5
- Blow Up — 6
- Going, Going, Gone — 8
- Eye to Eye — 10
- The Disappearing Shell — 12
- Blow Your Top! — 13
- Ready, Set, Boil — 14
- Hanging Around — 15
- Bubble and Boil — 16
- Ice Cold — 17
- Rising Ice — 18
- Pet Fog — 19
- Sparkle and Shine — 20
- Homegrown Gems — 22
- Making Music — 23
- Crunch — 24
- Heart Throb — 26
- Pokey Potato — 28
- Marvelous Mist — 29
- Pressure Point — 30
- Water Power — 31
- Crazy Quarter — 32
- Skin Tight — 34
- A Remarkable Race — 35
- Fruit Power — 36
- States of Matter — 38
- Catch Your Breath — 40
- Starch Detective — 41
- The Nose Knows — 42
- Brrrrr — 44
- Bubble Up — 46
- Drop by Drop — 48
- Gooey Moo — 50
- A Wet Blanket — 52
- Out of Sight — 53
- Heat Wave — 54
- Say Cheese — 56
- Mining For Iron — 58
- A Chilly Experience — 60
- Currents of Color — 62
- Sink or Float — 63
- Oldie Moldy — 64
- Baked Ice Cream — 66
- Water Bag — 68
- Down the Spout — 69
- Slip and Slide — 70
- Sweet or Salty — 72
- Molecules on the Move — 73
- Making Mayonnaise — 74
- Fast Fall — 76
- A Matter of Balance — 78
- Soak it Up — 79
- Secret Message — 80
- Cling, Cling, Cling — 82
- Lightning Strikes — 84
- Rockets Away! — 86
- Special Spoons — 87
- Temperature Trouble — 88
- Float and Sink — 90
- All Dried Up — 92
- Two or Three — 93
- Slip and Slide — 94
- Going Up — 96

Getting Started in the Kitchen

How does a straw work? What happens when you mix baking soda and vinegar? How much sugar can you stir into a full glass of water? The answers to these questions and more are as near as your own kitchen. With a few simple materials, you can test the chemical composition of a potato, remove the shell from a raw egg without touching it, and turn milk into plastic.

Here are some basic safety tips:

- Before you begin, read the directions completely.
- Wear old clothing or an apron.
- Never put an unknown material into your mouth or near your eyes.
- Label any long-term experiments that will be kept in your refrigerator or freezer.
- Use padded gloves when working with hot water.
- Clean up your work area.
- Wash your hands when you are finished.

You may need an adult helper for some of the experiments in this book. Most of the materials you'll need for these experiments are probably already in your home. Check with an adult before you use any household supplies.

Lights Out

Certain substances create strange chemical reactions when they combine. Some chemical reactions can be very useful.

Materials

- saucer
- clay
- candle
- matches
- drinking glass
- 2 tablespoons baking soda
- $\frac{1}{4}$ cup vinegar
- cardboard tube from a roll of toilet paper

Directions

❶ Press a walnut-sized ball of clay into the center of the saucer. Stand up the candle in the center of the clay. Ask an adult to light the candle.

❷ In the glass, mix 2 tablespoons of baking soda and $\frac{1}{4}$ cup of vinegar to create carbon dioxide gas.

❸ Quickly, hold the cardboard tube near—but not touching— the candle flame. Tip the glass as if you were pouring the invisible carbon dioxide gas through the tube and over the candle like water. Be careful not to pour out any of the baking soda-vinegar mixture. What happens to the flame?

Action, Reaction, Results

Fire uses oxygen in the air as fuel. By combining baking soda and vinegar, you begin a chemical reaction that produces carbon dioxide gas. Carbon dioxide gas is heavier than air. That is why you can pour it through the tube and over the candle flame. The gas replaces the air around the flame and extinguishes it.

Something Extra
Carbon dioxide gas will not burn. Many fire extinguishers work by pumping foam over flames. The foam is a blanket of bubbles of carbon dioxide gas.

Blow Up

Here's a way to blow up a balloon without using a single breath.

Materials

- plastic 12-ounce soda bottle
- petroleum jelly
- tissue paper
- 1 tablespoon baking soda
- $\frac{1}{2}$ cup vinegar
- balloon with a neck large enough to slip tightly over the opening of the soda bottle

Directions

❶ Lightly coat the rim of the soda bottle with petroleum jelly.

❷ Tear a piece of tissue about 2 inches square. Place a tablespoon of baking soda onto the tissue. Roll the tissue into a tube around the baking soda and twist the ends closed.

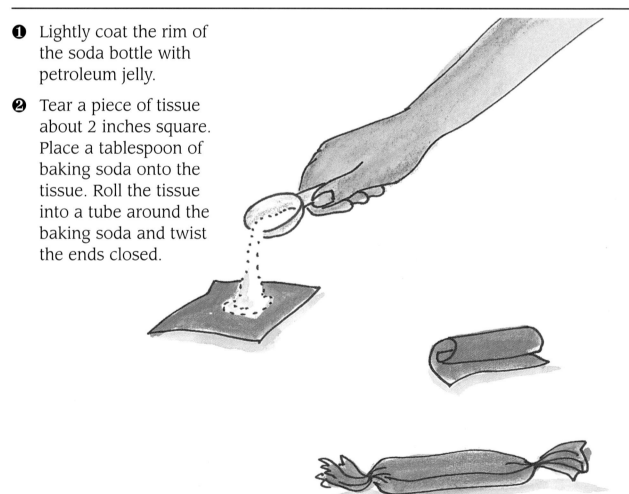

❸ Pour the vinegar into the soda bottle. Drop the baking soda packet into the bottle.

❹ Moving quickly, slip the neck of the balloon over the opening of the bottle and hold it in place. What happens?

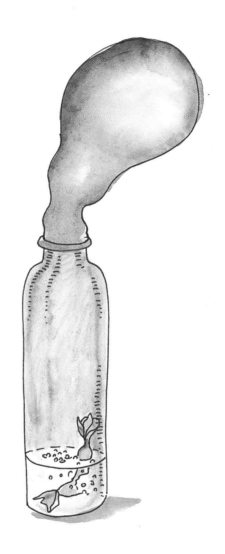

Action, Reaction, Results

When the tissue paper tears and the baking soda and vinegar meet, a chemical reaction takes place. Carbon dioxide, a gas, is produced. The gas expands out of the bottle and into the balloon, blowing it up.

WORD FILE

- **Expand:** To increase in size or volume.
- **Gas:** A state of matter, such as air, that has no definite shape, but takes the shape of the container it is in.

Going, Going, Gone

If you *mix*
Mix a cup of sugar into a cup of water and you'll have two cups of fluid. Right?
Maybe not.

Materials

- glass quart jar
- 2 measuring cups
- water
- marker
- spoon
- sugar

Directions

❶ Prepare the jar by filling it with 1 cup of water. Mark the water level with the marker. Pour in a second cup of water and mark the level. Empty the jar.

❷ Pour 1 cup of water into the jar. It should come to the level of the first mark.

❸ Pour 1 cup of sugar into the jar and stir. Does the solution reach the level of the second mark? Where did the sugar go?

Action, Reaction, Results

You can't see it, but there is plenty of space in the jar of water. The space is in between the water molecules. As you stir in the sugar, it dissolves and the sugar molecules slip into the spaces between the water molecules. Because of this, a cup of sugar stirred into a cup of water will measure less than two cups.

Eye to Eye

It's fun to plant a seed and watch it sprout and grow. Here's a way to enjoy a newly sprouting plant without planting a seed.

Materials

- potato
- knife
- small clay pot with saucer
- potting soil
- water

Directions

❶ Look for an "eye" on the potato. It is a small, round spot that is slightly rough to the touch.

❷ Ask an adult helper to cut a 1-inch square from the potato that includes an eye.

❸ Fill the clay pot with potting soil. Plant the square of potato 1 inch deep with the eye at the top. Cover it loosely with soil. Put the pot on a saucer. Water the soil until it is damp but not soaking.

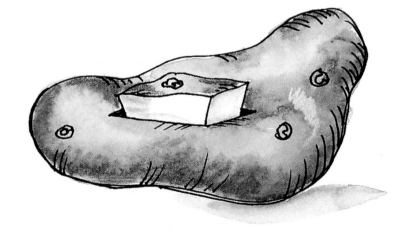

❹ Place the pot and saucer in a warm, sunny spot. Over the next 2 weeks, keep the soil moist and watch for your new plant to sprout.

Action, Reaction, Results

You don't always need seeds to grow a new plant. Many plants can grow from some part of a parent plant, such as a leaf, stem, or root. This is called vegetative propagation. A potato is a tuber, the swollen end of an underground stem. There are tiny buds and scale leaves on the tuber that can each sprout into a new plant. The potato itself is the food source for the sprout as it grows.

WORD FILE

- **Root:** A plant part that grows down into the soil and doesn't have leaves or buds. It anchors the plant in place and absorbs water and minerals from the soil.
- **Seed:** A small, self-contained body, produced by a flowering plant, that can sprout under proper conditions.
- **Stem:** The part of a plant that bears leaves and stems.

Something Extra

Potatoes can also be grown from seeds. Some farmers prefer to use the eyes of the potato, called sets, because the result is more predictable than with a seed-grown crop.

The Disappearing Shell

It may seem impossible to peel a raw egg, but it can be done. This experiment will show you how to use a "chemical peel."

Materials

- raw egg
- glass quart jar with lid
- vinegar

Directions

❶ Carefully place the egg into the glass jar.

❷ Fill the jar three-fourths full with vinegar.

❸ Observe the egg after 2 hours. Are bubbles forming?

❹ Leave the jar undisturbed for 3 days, checking occasionally.

❺ After 3 days, remove the lid, place your hand over the jar opening, and slowly pour the vinegar into a sink. Carefully allow the egg to slip into your hand. Handle it very gently as you observe it because it will break easily. How is the egg different? What is missing?

Action, Reaction, Results

By the end of this experiment, the shell of the egg is dissolved due to a chemical reaction between the shell and the vinegar. The shell is made of calcium carbonate that breaks down and creates carbon dioxide gas when exposed to vinegar, a mild acid. You see the bubbles of gas forming on the eggshell. The bubbling continues until the eggshell is completely used up.

WORD FILE

- **Chemical reaction:** A chemical change that occurs when two or more substances interact with each other.
- **Dissolve:** To make a solid or gas disappear into a liquid.

Blow Your Top!

Be a kitchen chemist—use baking soda and vinegar to create an amazing chemical reaction.

Materials

- spoon
- $\frac{1}{2}$ cup water
- $\frac{1}{2}$ cup vinegar
- $\frac{1}{4}$ cup dishwashing liquid
- two glass pint jars
- $\frac{1}{4}$ cup baking soda
- medium-sized mixing bowl

Directions

❶ Stir the water, vinegar, and dishwashing liquid together in one jar.

❷ Put the baking soda in the other jar. Place that jar in the bowl to catch any spillover.

❸ Pour the contents of the first jar into the second jar. Stir quickly and watch.

Action, Reaction, Results

Baking soda is a base. Vinegar is an acid. When a base and an acid are combined, they create a chemical reaction. In a chemical reaction, molecules interact to create new molecules. Together, the baking soda and vinegar produce carbon dioxide gas.

Something Extra

Here's a way to really raise a reaction. In a 9- by 13-inch shallow baking dish, make a volcano from dirt, damp sand, or papier-mâché. Mold the shape with a pocket at the top to hold the jar of baking soda. Repeat the experiment above, and watch your volcano erupt!

Ready, Set, Boil

You've probably heard the old saying, "A watched pot never boils." What about a salted pot?

Materials

- 2 small pots
- cold water
- 3 tablespoons salt
- spoon
- stove

Directions

❶ Fill each pot halfway with water.

❷ Add 3 tablespoons of salt to the first pot.

❸ Place each pot on a burner on the stove. Ask an adult to supervise as you turn each burner on high.

❹ Wait for the water to boil. Which pot starts to boil first?

❺ Note the time that the first pot boils. How much longer does it take before the second pot boils?

Action, Reaction, Results

The unsalted water reaches its boiling point first. The salt molecules in the salty water have a higher boiling point than water, so they interfere with the process. It takes longer because the salted water must reach a higher temperature before it will boil.

> **WORD FILE**
>
> - **Boiling point:** The point at which something changes from a liquid to a gas or vapor.
> - **Molecule:** The smallest unit of a material that still has the characteristics of that material.

Something Extra

Salting the water when you are cooking can speed up your cooking time because the water boils at a higher temperature.

Hanging Around

Can you pick up an ice cube with a string? This surprising experiment will show you how.

Materials

- drinking glass
- water
- ice cube
- 4-inch piece of string
- salt

Directions

❶ Fill the glass nearly to the top with water.

❷ Float an ice cube in the water. Hold the string at one end and drape the other end across the ice cube.

❸ Sprinkle a pinch of salt around the end of the string that is on the ice cube.

❹ Count slowly to 10, then pull on the end of the string that you are holding to lift the ice cube out of the water.

Action, Reaction, Results

Water freezes at 32 degrees Fahrenheit. Salt water freezes at a lower temperature than that. By sprinkling salt on the ice cube, you lower its melting point, causing it to melt slightly around the string. The fluid that flows under the string quickly turns to ice again, freezing the string in place.

Bubble and Boil

Which has a lower boiling point, fresh water or salt water? It will only take you a few minutes to find out.

Materials

- two 1- or 2-quart pots
- water
- spoon
- 3 tablespoons salt
- stove

Directions

❶ Fill each pot with 2 cups water.

❷ Stir the salt into one of the pots of water.

❸ Ask an adult observer to stand by as you place both pots on the stove and bring each to a boil. Which one boils first?

❹ Use a kitchen timer, or a clock or watch with a second hand, to determine how much longer it takes for the second pot of water to come to a boil.

Action, Reaction, Results

The fresh water boils first. Matter is made up of tiny units called atoms. Some atoms join together to form larger units called molecules. The molecules of salt in the salt water distribute themselves throughout the water and interfere with the boiling process, raising the water's boiling point.

Ice Cold

All materials have a freezing point. Can the freezing point be changed?

Materials

- coffee can
- crushed ice
- cold water
- outdoor thermometer
- spoon
- 2 tablespoons salt

Directions

❶ Fill the coffee can halfway with crushed ice. Add enough cold water to cover the ice.

❷ Wait a minute, then dunk the thermometer into the ice. After another minute, read the temperature.

❸ Remove the thermometer and stir the salt into the ice water in the can.

❹ Dunk the thermometer into the can again. Wait a minute, then read the temperature. Is it different?

Action, Reaction, Results

The temperature of the salt water is lower. The freezing point for fresh water is 32 degrees Fahrenheit. When water freezes, the molecules in the water line up in a certain way. When you add salt to the water, the salt molecules interfere with the freezing process. Heat energy is used up as the salt dissolves, and the temperature drops. Salt water doesn't freeze until the temperature reaches about 28.6 degrees Fahrenheit.

Rising Ice

Most substances contract when they freeze, but not water.

Materials

- pint jar
- clay
- plastic straw
- measuring cup
- water
- food coloring
- marker

Directions

❶ Press a walnut-sized ball of clay inside the jar at the center of the bottom.

❷ Stick the straw firmly into the clay so that it stands straight up.

❸ Mix a few drops of food coloring into $\frac{1}{2}$ cup of water, then slowly pour the water into the straw until it is half filled. Don't worry if some spills. Mark the water level on the straw with a marker. Place the jar in the freezer.

❹ After 4 hours the water will be frozen. Check the level of the ice in the straw. Is it higher?

Action, Reaction, Results

Water has some unusual properties. Unlike most substances, water expands when it reaches its freezing point. When frozen, the water molecules join together in a hexagonal structure that takes up more space than water molecules do in liquid form.

WORD FILE

- **Freezing point:** The point at which a liquid becomes a solid.
- **Hexagonal:** Having a six-sided shape.

Pet Fog

Fog is simply a ground-hugging cloud. Here's how to create your own fog in a bottle.

Materials

- empty 2-liter soda bottle with no cap
- very warm water
- large ice cube

Directions

❶ Fill the bottle with very warm water to heat the air inside. Let it sit for a minute.

❷ Pour out all but an inch of the water.

❸ Place the ice cube over the neck of the bottle so that it completely covers the opening.

Action, Reaction, Results

The warm air inside the bottle contains water vapor. The water vapor cools when ice is placed on top of the bottle. It condenses into tiny droplets, which look much like fog.

Something Extra
Try this experiment again, but this time wrap the ice in plastic wrap.

Sparkle and Shine

Certain substances are made of crystals, glasslike solids with regular shapes. With this experiment, you can have fun while creating your own crop of crystals.

Materials

- teacup
- scissors
- black construction paper
- measuring cup
- salt
- water
- spoon

Directions

❶ Cut a shape (such as a flower, an animal, or a star) from the black construction paper. Be sure it fits and will stand up in the teacup. Place the construction paper cutout inside the cup in an upright position.

❷ Mix salt into ½ cup of water. Keep adding salt until no more will dissolve.

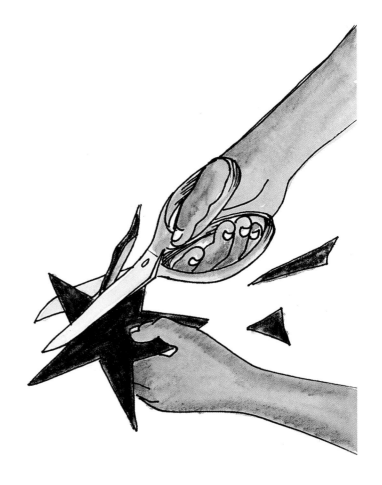

❸ Fill the teacup with about $\frac{1}{2}$ inch of salty water. Keep the cutout standing up. Set the cup in a warm, dry place. Let it remain undisturbed for 3 days or until all the water has evaporated. What has been left behind on the construction paper?

Action, Reaction, Results

The salty water moves up through the construction paper by capillary action. Tiny fibers that make up the paper have spaces between them. Water molecules move through the spaces by adhering to the fibers. As the water molecules move up, they attract and draw up water molecules from below. As the water in the construction paper dries, it leaves behind deposits of salt crystals, particularly along the upper edge of the paper.

WORD FILE
• **Evaporate:** To change from a liquid to a gas or vapor. • **Fibers:** Threadlike structures.

Homegrown Gems

Things don't have to be alive to grow. You can grow your own garden of gems in a jar.

Materials

- glass quart jar
- warm water
- alum (available in supermarkets)
- spoon
- pencil
- 10 inches of nylon thread
- paper clip

Directions

❶ Fill the jar with warm water to within an inch of the top.

❷ Stir in the alum until no more will dissolve.

❸ Tie the string around the center of the pencil.

❹ Tie a paper clip to the other end of the string. Lower the paper clip into the jar. Rest the pencil across the top of the jar. Turn the pencil to shorten the string until the paper clip hangs an inch from the bottom.

❺ Place the jar in a warm, sunny place where it will be undisturbed. Check on the progress every day or two as your crystals grow.

Action, Reaction, Results

The molecules that make up crystals form a definite structure. By stirring alum into the warm water you create a solution. As the water evaporates, the molecules realign and produce crystals that cling to the string and sides of the jar. The crystals continue to form until all of the solution has evaporated.

WORD FILE

- **Alum:** A chemical salt used in pickling.
- **Evaporate:** To convert to vapor or to pass off moisture.
- **Solution:** One or more substances dissolved in another substance, usually liquid.

Making Music

How would you like to put on a little concert in your kitchen? Here's a way to make and play your own musical instrument.

Materials

- six 12-ounce glass soda bottles
- water
- spoon

Directions

❶ Line up the soda bottles on a flat surface with 2 inches of space between them.

❷ Fill the first bottle with about $\frac{1}{2}$ inch of water. Fill the next bottle $\frac{1}{2}$ inch higher than the first. Continue to fill each bottle $\frac{1}{2}$ inch higher than the bottle before it.

❸ Holding the spoon loosely, tap each bottle near the top. Is there a difference in the sound that each bottle makes? Just for fun, try to tap out a tune.

Action, Reaction, Results

Sound is actually waves of vibrations. When you tap the bottles with the spoon you cause them to vibrate. The vibrations travel in waves through the air into your ear. You perceive the vibrations as sound. The number of vibrations is called the frequency of the sound. The bottle with the least amount of water vibrates the most and has the highest pitch. The bottle with the most water vibrates the least and has the lowest pitch.

WORD FILE

- **Pitch:** A characteristic of sound; a measure of the frequency of a vibration. A high frequency vibration produces a note of high pitch.
- **Vibration:** To move regularly backward and forward.

Crunch

At this moment air is pushing on you and everything around you. You usually don't notice it, but here's a way to see how powerful air can be.

Materials

- 1-liter plastic soda bottle with cap
- warm water
- 1 cup crushed ice
- funnel

Directions

❶ Fill the bottle with warm water and let it sit for 5 minutes.

❷ Empty the bottle. Use the funnel to pour 1 cup of crushed ice into the bottle as quickly as possible, then tightly screw on the cap.

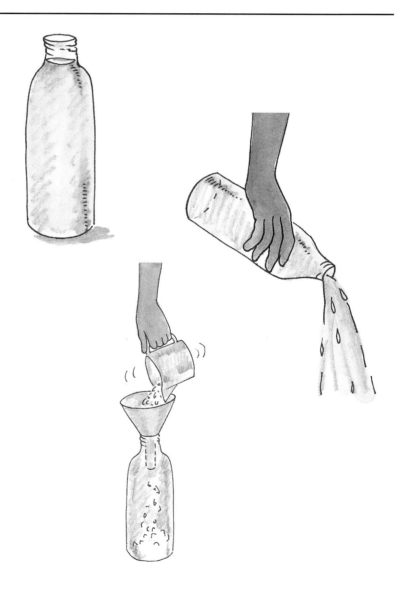

❸ Shake the bottle, then place it where it can remain undisturbed for at least 1 hour. What happens?

Action, Reaction, Results

Molecules of air spread out when they are heated and move together when they are chilled. By warming the air in the bottle with warm water, you cause the air inside to expand. When you put in the ice, you chill the air and it contracts and lowers the pressure inside the bottle. The air pressure outside the bottle is greater, so eventually the sides of the bottle collapse.

WORD FILE

- **Contract:** To become smaller in size or volume.
- **Expand:** To become larger in size or volume.

Heart Throb

If you like marshmallows, you'll see more than you bargained for with this experiment.

Materials

- small glass bottle with a small mouth (such as an empty aspirin bottle)
- miniature marshmallow
- sharp-pointed marker
- clay
- flexible straw
- mirror

Directions

❶ Draw a heart on the marshmallow and put it into the bottle. Place the marshmallow so that the heart is facing outward.

❷ Put about an inch of the straw into the bottle, then seal the opening of the bottle closed with clay. Use enough clay to seal it completely and hold the straw in place.

❸ Set up a mirror on a table so that you can watch the marshmallow as you perform the experiment.

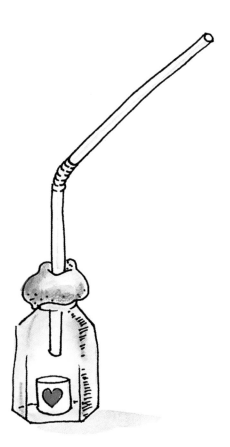

❹ Suck the air out of the bottle through the straw. Keep the straw in your mouth as you look in the mirror. What happens to the marshmallow?

❺ Release the straw to allow the air back into the bottle. Now what happens to the marshmallow?

Action, Reaction, Results

There is air all around everything, and it pushes in all directions. There is air in the bottle and in the marshmallow. When you suck out the air through the straw you lower the air pressure in the bottle. The air that is left expands to take up the available space. The air-filled marshmallow expands, too. As you watch in the mirror you can see the heart get bigger. When you allow the air back into the bottle, the marshmallow returns to its original size.

WORD FILE

- **Air pressure:** The pushing or squeezing force that air exerts on everything it touches.

Pokey Potato

Impress your friends by demonstrating the power of air pressure with this experiment.

Materials

- raw potato
- two plastic drinking straws

Directions

❶ Place the potato on a hard surface, such as a table. Hold the first straw vertically a few inches above the potato, so that neither opening is covered.

❷ Holding the potato in place with one hand, try to stab it with the straw. The straw will crumple and have little effect on the potato.

❸ Hold the second straw vertically a few inches above the potato. This time, cover the top opening with your thumb.

❹ Try to stab the potato again. What happens?

Action, Reaction, Results

Compressed air is air that is squeezed into a small space, such as a straw. Compressed air provides a lot of force because it is more dense and is under greater pressure than the air outside the straw. The air trapped inside the second straw made the straw strong enough to actually stab the potato.

Marvelous Mist

Plants often enjoy a spritz of water. Here's a way to make a simple mist sprayer that your plants will appreciate.

Materials

- drinking glass
- plant
- water
- 2 plastic straws
- scissors

Directions

❶ Set the glass next to the plant on a flat surface.

❷ Fill the glass with water.

❸ Trim one straw so that it is 1 inch higher than the rim of the glass.

❹ Facing the plant, hold the second straw at a right angle to the first straw. Blow gently through the second straw, and you will see the water level rise in the first.

❺ Blow very hard through the second straw. What happens?

Action, Reaction, Results

Air pressure pushes down on the water in the glass, pushing water up into the straw. As you blow into the second straw and across the first, you lower the air pressure over the first straw causing the water in it to rise. Once the water reaches the top of the straw, tiny droplets are carried by the gust of air you are blowing. The droplets reach the plant as a fine, cool mist.

Something Extra
Perfume often comes in a special bottle called an atomizer. The atomizer works much like the plant sprayer you made. It has a large, flexible bulb that creates airflow when it is squeezed, and that airflow helps to deliver a fine mist of perfume.

Pressure Point

As an ice skater glides across the ice, the pressure from the blades of the skates melts the ice beneath the blades. The skater actually glides on a thin layer of water.

Materials

- corked bottle
- ice cube
- $3\frac{1}{2}$-inch piece of strong, thin wire
- 2 heavy bolts

Directions

❶ Twist one end of the wire around the bolt. Twist the other end of the wire around the other bolt.

❷ With the cork in the bottle, balance the ice cube on the top of the cork. Drape the wire over the center of the ice cube.

❸ Put the bottle in the refrigerator and check it every 15 minutes until the wire is resting on the cork.

Action, Reaction, Results

The pressure of the wire melts the ice directly underneath it. The wire moves down through the water, which re-freezes behind it. The wire will travel slowly through the ice cube all the way to the cork, but it won't cut the cube in two.

WORD FILE

- **Pressure:** A pushing or squeezing force that works on a given area.

Water Power

Create a water fountain in your kitchen sink and learn about water pressure at the same time.

Materials

- empty $\frac{1}{2}$-gallon paper milk carton
- large nail
- masking tape
- water

Directions

❶ With the nail, make three holes in one side of the milk carton in line from top to bottom. Make the first hole 1 inch from the bottom and make the second and third holes in line above it, each 1 inch apart.

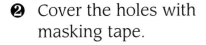

❷ Cover the holes with masking tape.

❸ Place the carton in the sink under the tap. Fill it with water.

❹ Remove the tape. The water will stream out. Which stream flows the farthest?

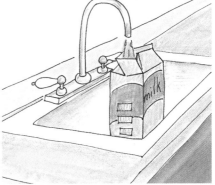

Action, Reaction, Results

Water has weight, and the weight creates pressure. The water in the carton pushes down and out against the sides of the carton. Because of the weight of the water above it, the water pressure is highest at the bottom of the carton, and that stream sprays farther than the others.

Crazy Quarter

When air gets cold, it contracts, or takes up less space. When air gets warm, it expands, or takes up more space.

Materials

- empty 2-liter soda bottle without a cap
- freezer
- flat surface
- water
- quarter

Directions

❶ Put the empty soda bottle in the freezer for at least 30 minutes.

❷ Take the bottle out of the freezer and place it on a flat surface.

❸ Wet the quarter and place it over the top of the open bottle. The quarter must completely cover the opening of the bottle.

❹ Put your hands around the sides of the bottle to warm it. Wait a few moments. What happens?

Action, Reaction, Results

When you put the bottle in the freezer, the air in the bottle became cold. The cold air contracted, or shrank. When you removed the bottle from the freezer and held it, the air inside the bottle became warmer. The warm air expanded, or spread out, increasing the pressure in the bottle. The expanding air pushed out and up. The quarter covered the top of the bottle, so the air pushed up on the quarter. The quarter jumped, and a little air escaped. This released some of the pressure. As the air in the bottle continued to warm up, it pushed on the quarter again and again, making the quarter "dance."

Something Extra
Prepare a large bowl of cold water filled with ice cubes. Ask an adult to help you fill an empty 2-liter soda bottle with very hot tap water. Leave the water in the bottle for three minutes, then pour it out. Stretch the open end of a balloon over the mouth of the bottle. Put the bottle into the icy cold water. The balloon will enter the bottle and inflate. Why do you think this happens?

Skin Tight

Water has a stretchy skin. In this experiment, you will demonstrate a property of that unusual skin.

Materials

- bowl at least 8 inches across
- water
- 7 wooden toothpicks
- dishwashing soap

Directions

❶ Set the bowl on a flat surface and fill it with water. Wait for the water to stop moving.

❷ Carefully arrange six toothpicks on the surface of the water with their tips pointing toward the center in a "sunburst" pattern. Use the other toothpick to move them around.

❸ Squirt a drop of dishwashing soap into the water at the center of the bowl. What happens?

Action, Reaction, Results

Molecules near the surface of the water have a tendency to "cling" to each other creating a stretchy "skin" called surface tension. The toothpicks float on the skin. Putting the drop of soap in the center weakens the cling at that point. The skin is drawn to the edges of the bowl, and the toothpicks are drawn along with it.

Something Extra
The water strider is an insect that spends most of its time on water. This lightweight creature doesn't sink because it is supported by surface tension.

A Remarkable Race

Get ready to race with this unusual form of power, created when detergent disrupts the surface tension of water.

Materials

- large bowl
- water
- scissors
- piece of lightweight cardboard
- dishwashing liquid

Directions

❶ Fill the bowl nearly to the rim with water.

❷ Cut a small triangle from the cardboard, about 1 inch wide on each side. Cut out a small notch on one side of the triangle. This is your "boat."

❸ Gently lay the boat flat on the surface of the water. The notch should be near the edge of the bowl.

❹ Carefully place a drop of dishwashing liquid in the water where the notch is. Watch the boat take off!

Action, Reaction, Results

The molecules of the dishwashing liquid are attracted to the molecules of the water. This attraction disrupts the cohesion of the water molecules. When you place the drop of dishwashing liquid on the water, it breaks the surface tension, causing a ripple effect that forces the boat forward.

Something Extra
Another simple way to see the effect of dishwashing liquid on surface tension is to sprinkle pepper over the surface of a bowl of water. Place a drop of dishwashing liquid in the center of the bowl and watch the pepper move away from the center and toward the edge of the bowl.

Fruit Power

If your flashlight batteries go dim, you may be able to find a replacement in the fruit drawer of your refrigerator.

Materials

- lemon
- brass thumbtack
- steel paper clip
- two 6-inch pieces of electrical wire
- low-voltage flashlight bulb
- small knife

Directions

❶ Ask an adult to strip $1\frac{1}{2}$ inches of insulation from both ends of each piece of electrical wire with the small knife.

❷ Take one piece of wire and wrap one end around the brass tack and the other end around the base of the flashlight bulb. Take the second piece of wire and wrap one end around the paper clip and the other end around the base of the flashlight bulb.

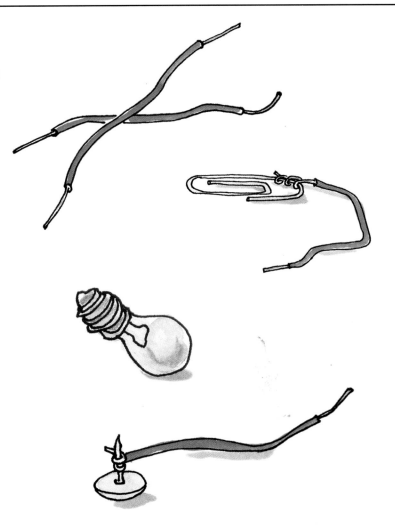

❸ Insert both the brass
  tack and the paper clip
  into lemon, as shown.
  What happens?

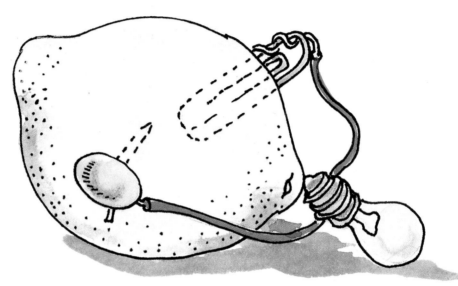

Action, Reaction, Results

Electricity is generated when materials combine and create chemical reactions. A battery is a portable method of providing electricity. In a battery, there is a chemical called an electrolyte between two metal electrodes. In this demonstration, the acid in the lemon acts as the electrolyte and reacts with the metal in the tack and paper clip which act as electrodes. When the lemon, electrical wire, and bulb are connected, they create an electrical circuit that makes the bulb light up.

Something Extra

Batteries are used in many ways. Look around your own home and count any items that may be battery powered. Don't forget radios, clocks, and toys. How many can you find?

States of Matter

Everything in the universe, from the smallest ant to the largest star, is made of matter. Matter comes in three states, or forms: solid, liquid, and gas.

Materials

- three ice cubes
- self-sealing sandwich bag
- microwave-safe dish
- microwave oven

Directions

❶ Put the ice cubes into the sandwich bag. Seal the bag.

❷ Place the bag on a microwave-safe dish. Put the dish inside the microwave oven.

❸ Ask an adult to help you heat the bag for 90 seconds at high power. If the ice isn't completely melted, heat the bag for another 30 seconds. The ice will form water.

❹ Now heat the bag for another 30 seconds. What happens? Why?

❺ Let the bag cool completely before removing it from the microwave.

Experiments You Can Do in Your Kitchen

Action, Reaction, Results

In this experiment, matter changed its state, or form. Solid ice became liquid water, then a gas called water vapor. This happened because the molecules, or particles, of matter were heated up. The molecules of matter are always moving around. In a solid, like ice, the molecules are close together and move very slowly. When a solid is heated, the molecules move farther apart. The solid becomes a liquid. When a liquid is heated, the molecules move even faster and farther apart, becoming a gas. Your bag puffed up because the water became water vapor. The gas molecules moved farther apart, filling more space in the bag. Matter can also change its state in the other direction. When a gas is cooled enough, it can become a liquid, then a solid.

Something Extra

When you finish the experiment, put the bag in the freezer. Check it after three or four hours. What happens to the bag? Why?

Catch Your Breath

With two straws in your mouth and one in a glass of water, can you still drink?

Materials

- drinking glass
- water
- 2 straws

Directions

❶ Place the glass on a flat surface and fill it to the rim with water.

❷ Place both straws in your mouth.

❸ Put one straw into the water-filled glass and let the other straw remain outside the glass.

❹ Try to draw in a drink of water through the straw that is in the glass.

Action, Reaction, Results

When you drink through a straw, you lower the pressure in your mouth and create a partial vacuum. The outside air pressure pushes down on the fluid in the glass and forces it up the straw. By sucking through two straws (one in the liquid and one in the air), you can't form a partial vacuum. The straw in the air creates a leak. The air pressure in your mouth remains the same as that outside, and no liquid is forced up the straw. The fluid remains in the glass.

WORD FILE

- **Vacuum:** A space that is completely empty with no molecules of any kind in it.

Starch Detective

Starch, as a carbohydrate, can be an important part of the human diet. In this experiment, you can make starch show up in a common food.

Materials

- peeled potato
- grater
- strainer
- paper towel
- salt
- tincture of iodine

Directions

❶ Grate a tablespoon of potato into a strainer.

❷ Press the potato through the strainer onto a paper towel to make a small pile of mushy potato. Place $\frac{1}{4}$ teaspoon of salt on the paper towel near the potato.

❸ Place 2 drops of tincture of iodine on the salt, then 2 drops on the potato. What do you see?

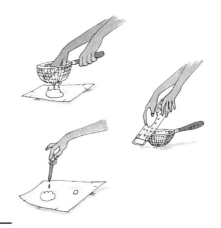

Action, Reaction, Results

Due to a chemical reaction, iodine turns blue-black in the presence of starch. The drop of iodine on the salt does not change color because there is no starch in the salt. The drop of iodine on the potato turns blue-black. Starch is a carbohydrate that is converted by the body to simple sugars and used as fuel.

WORD FILE

- **Carbohydrate:** A compound made up of carbon, hydrogen, and oxygen.

Something Extra

Plants store some of the food they make during photosynthesis as starch. The starch may be stored in seeds and stems or roots and underground stems, as in the case of the potato. Foods containing starch can help fuel your energy.

The Nose Knows

A bad cold can ruin your appetite. That's partly because when your nose is stuffed up, you can't smell your food. Your nose is your mouth's partner when it's time to taste.

Materials

- peeled apple
- peeled raw potato
- grater
- 2 identical small bowls
- stick-on labels
- marker

Directions

❶ Grate a small amount of apple and put it into a bowl. Grate a small amount of potato and put it into the second bowl. Label each bowl on the bottom so that you can only see it by lifting the bowl.

❷ Close your eyes and mix up the bowls so that you can't tell which is which.

❸ Hold your nose and taste the food from each bowl. Can you taste which is which?

❹ Taste each food without holding your nose. Is it easier to taste the difference?

Action, Reaction, Results

The sense of smell and sense of taste work together. The nose and mouth share the same airway—the pharynx. The tastebuds on the tongue and palate can determine whether something is sweet, salty, bitter, or sour. The odor of a food helps you to distinguish more subtle flavors.

WORD FILE

- **Pharynx:** A cavity at the back of the mouth where the oral and nasal cavities meet.
- **Tastebuds:** Tiny bodies that contain receptors that gather and send taste information to the brain.

Brrrrr

Can anything be colder than ice? Check out this experiment and decide for yourself.

Materials

- coffee can
- crushed ice
- water
- outdoor thermometer
- salt
- spoon

Directions

❶ Fill the coffee can halfway with crushed ice. Add water to cover the ice.

❷ Place the thermometer in the can. Wait 1 minute, then read the temperature.

❸ Stir in 2 teaspoons of salt. Wait 1 minute, then read the temperature again. Did it change?

Action, Reaction, Results

Plain, unsalted water freezes at 32 degrees Fahrenheit. Salt lowers the freezing point of water. In this experiment, heat energy from the water is used up as the salt dissolves. As heat is removed from the water, the temperature drops. Salt water freezes at about 28.6 degrees Fahrenheit.

WORD FILE

• **Freezing point:** The point at which a liquid becomes a solid.

Bubble Up

Do you like sugar? A common fungus also uses sugar as food. Most plants make their own food. This experiment will help you learn about those that don't.

Materials

- 1 package powdered yeast
- 1 tablespoon sugar
- measuring cup
- 12-ounce glass soda bottle
- warm water
- balloon (with neck large enough to fit tightly over the bottle opening)

Directions

❶ Mix the yeast and sugar into 1 cup of warm water. Pour the fluid into the glass bottle.

❷ Slip the neck of the balloon over the opening of the bottle.

❸ Place the bottle in a dark, warm place where it will not be disturbed. Check the bottle after 1 hour. What has happened?

❹ Check the bottle again after 12 hours. What has happened? Check one final time after 24 hours.

Action, Reaction, Results

Green plants use chlorophyll in their food-making process. Some plants called fungi do not have chlorophyll. Yeast is a fungus. It uses food, such as sugar, as fuel. During the process, carbon dioxide gas is produced. The bubbles you see in the bottle during the experiment are carbon dioxide gas. The gas expands and fills the balloon.

- **Chlorophyll:** A green substance in plants used to convert sunlight, air, and water into food.
- **Expands:** To get larger in size or volume.
- **Fungi:** Plural of fungus.
- **Fungus:** A single-celled or threadlike plant that contains no chlorophyll.

Something Extra

Some fungi cause disease and can be dangerous. Others are helpful. Certain fungi feed on dead organisms and help to get rid of them. Yeast is a fungus used to bake bread. It feeds on the sugar in the dough and produces carbon dioxide gas that causes the bread to rise.

Drop by Drop

Surprise your friends with this remarkable demonstration of attraction.

Materials

- waxed paper
- cup of water
- straw
- toothpick

Directions

❶ Place a sheet of waxed paper on a flat surface.

❷ Dip one end of the straw into the cup of water. Place your thumb over the open end of the straw and lift it out of the water. A droplet will be trapped in the straw.

❸ Lift your thumb to release the trapped droplet onto the waxed paper. Make three more drops.

❹ Wet the toothpick in the cup of water, then hold it very near—but not touching—one of the drops on the waxed paper. What happens to the drop? Try using the toothpick to drag a drop across the waxed paper. What happens when one drop meets another?

Action, Reaction, Results

Water molecules are attracted to each other. Because of this, the drops are attracted to each other and to the water on the toothpick. This attractive force is called cohesion.

WORD FILE

- **Cohesion:** Attractive force between molecules of the same type.
- **Molecule:** The smallest unit of a material that still has the characteristics of that material.

Gooey Moo

That milk in your refrigerator can take a totally different and fun form.

Materials

- 1 cup whole milk
- saucepan
- $\frac{1}{2}$ cup vinegar
- stove

Directions

❶ Pour the milk into a saucepan. Ask an adult to help you warm the milk to a slow boil.

❷ Add the vinegar and stir slowly until the mixture becomes rubbery.

❸ Let the material cool, then rinse it under cool running water. What does it remind you of? What can you do with it?

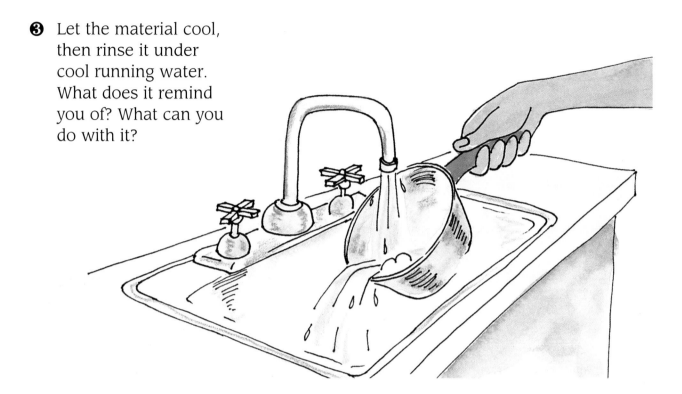

Action, Reaction, Results

Milk contains a substance called carbon, which reacts with the acid in the vinegar. The result is a plasticlike substance that can be molded into shapes and even bounced.

WORD FILE

- **Carbon:** An element. Carbon compounds are found in many plants and animals.

A Wet Blanket

Can ice help to keep you warm? The answer may surprise you.

Materials

- two pieces of aluminum foil
- two outdoor thermometers
- paper towels
- water
- two saucers
- freezer

Directions

❶ Fold the aluminum foil to make two loose pockets. Leave an opening at one end of each pocket so the thermometers can slip in and out.

❷ Put a thermometer in each pocket. Soak one of the paper towels with water, then wrap it around one foil pocket. Wrap a dry paper towel around the outside of the other pocket.

❸ Lay one pocket on each saucer. Place both in the freezer. Check the temperature of each thermometer every 5 minutes for 20 minutes. Does one stay warmer?

Action, Reaction, Results

As water begins to freeze, it gives off energy in the form of heat. When the wet paper towel begins to freeze, it warms the air around the thermometer just a little, so the temperature is slightly higher than that on the other thermometer. Once the water on the paper towel has frozen, the air begins to cool again.

Out of Sight

Be a kitchen chemist. Use baking soda and vinegar to create an amazing chemical reaction.

Materials

- two thumbtacks
- two small paper cups
- wooden ruler
- two empty soda cans
- $\frac{1}{4}$ cup vinegar
- drinking glass
- 1 tablespoon baking soda
- spoon

Directions

❶ Tack a paper cup to each end of the ruler.

❷ Set one soda can upright on a table. Place another can on its side on top of the first. Balance the ruler on the top can so that it is level.

❸ Pour vinegar into the drinking glass, then mix in the baking soda.

❹ As the mixture begins to foam, tilt the glass over one of the paper cups tacked to the end of the ruler. Be careful not to touch the cup or pour any of the foaming liquid into it. Does the cup move?

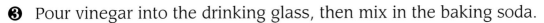

Action, Reaction, Results

A chemical reaction is what takes place when two or more chemical elements combine to form something else. When mixed together, baking soda and vinegar combine to produce carbon dioxide gas. The gas is heavier than air. Although you cannot see it, the carbon dioxide gas pours into the cup, adding weight and unbalancing the ruler.

Something Extra

To see the carbon dioxide gas, perform your experiment outside in a sunny spot. Hold a large piece of white poster board behind the glass as you pour out the invisible gas. The gas will bend the light rays that pass through it, and you will see faint shadows on the board.

Heat Wave

When you leave certain metal objects out in the rain, a chemical reaction takes place. Rust is the product of that reaction.

Materials

- glass jar with lid
- outdoor thermometer to fit in the jar
- 1 soap-free steel wool scouring pad
- vinegar
- bowl

Directions

❶ Put the thermometer in the jar and close the lid. Wait 5 minutes, then note the temperature.

❷ Pull the steel wool pad apart to loosen the fibers. Place it in the bowl and cover it with vinegar. Wait 5 minutes.

❸ Take the steel wool out of the vinegar and allow it to drain. Remove the thermometer from the jar. Wrap the steel wool around the bulb of the thermometer, put it back into the jar, and replace the lid.

❹ Wait 5 minutes, then note the temperature again.

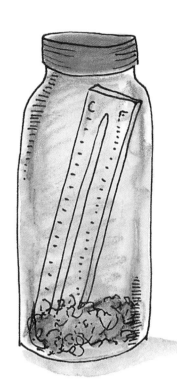

Action, Reaction, Results

The temperature rises after you put the steel wool into the jar. By soaking the steel wool in the vinegar you remove any coating. The iron in the steel begins to oxidize and produce rust. The process produces heat, which causes the temperature in the jar to rise.

WORD FILE

- **Oxidize:** To add oxygen to a substance.
- **Rust:** A reddish-colored coating of oxidized iron.

Say Cheese

Mix lemon juice with milk and you'll create a gooey mess, that is, unless you heat it first.

Materials

- 2 tablespoons lemon juice
- cup
- saucepan
- 1 quart milk
- wooden spoon
- cheesecloth
- colander
- small bowl
- stove

Directions

❶ Pour 2 tablespoons of lemon juice into a cup.

❷ With an adult helper, pour the milk into the saucepan and turn on the burner to medium-high. Stir slowly with a wooden spoon and watch for small bubbles to form.

❸ Once the milk begins to boil, remove the pan from the stove. Stir in the lemon juice.

❹ Return the saucepan to the stove and continue to stir on medium heat until lumps begin to form. Turn off the stove, remove the saucepan from the burner, and allow the mixture to cool for 5 minutes.

❺ Place the colander in the sink, line it with cheesecloth, and pour the mixture into it. The lumps, called curds, will collect in the bottom.

❻ Once the liquid has drained away, put the curds into a small bowl and refrigerate. You might want to add a little salt before you eat this cheese.

Action, Reaction, Results

Adding lemon juice, a mild acid, to warmed milk causes the protein in the milk to form lumps, or to coagulate. The end result is a homemade form of cottage cheese.

WORD FILE

- **Coagulate:** To thicken.
- **Protein:** Substance made up of hundreds or even thousands of simpler units linked together called amino acids. Amino acids contain carbon, hydrogen, oxygen, nitrogen, and sometimes sulfur.

Mining for Iron

Have you heard of people having muscles of steel? Maybe it's because they get so much iron in their fruit juice.

Materials

- pint glass jar
- 4 tea bags
- water
- 3 small glasses
- measuring cup
- pineapple juice, white grape juice, apple juice
- 3 plastic spoons

Directions

❶ Put all four tea bags into the jar and fill it to the top with warm water. Let the jar sit for 2 hours.

❷ Pour $\frac{1}{4}$ cup of tea solution into each of the three glasses.

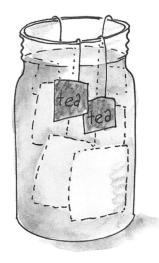

❸ Rinsing the measuring cup after each juice, pour ¼ cup of pineapple juice into the first glass, ¼ cup of white grape juice into the second glass, and ¼ cup of apple juice into the third glass.

❹ Let the glasses sit for 30 minutes, then lift each glass and check to see if any dark particles have settled on the bottom.

❺ Let the glasses sit for another 2 hours, then check again for dark particles.

Action, Reaction, Results

A chemical reaction takes place when chemicals in the tea come in contact with iron in the juice. Dark particles form and settle to the bottom of the glass. The pineapple juice contains a lot of iron so a lot of particles form quickly. It takes longer for particles to develop in the white grape juice. No particles develop in the apple juice because it does not contain iron.

Something Extra

Iron is important in the human body for several reasons. Iron is what makes blood red and enables blood to carry oxygen. Iron also plays an important part in the liver in breaking down toxins.

A Chilly Experience

The density of air varies with the temperature. Is it warmer near the floor or the ceiling in your home? Try this experiment, then think about the answer.

Materials

- seven ice cubes
- 1 teaspoon salt
- zip-top sandwich bag
- two pencils, sharpened
- empty oatmeal box, lid removed
- outdoor thermometer
- tape

Directions

❶ Put the ice cubes and salt in the sandwich bag, then seal the bag.

❷ Use one pencil to make a thermometer-sized hole in the side of the oatmeal box about $\frac{1}{2}$ inch from the bottom. Insert the thermometer about halfway in. Note the temperature.

❸ Set both pencils side by side across the top of the oatmeal box with a small space between them, then tape them in place. Balance the bag of ice and salt on top of the pencils.

❹ Wait 15 minutes, then read the temperature on the thermometer again.

Action, Reaction, Results

Cold air is more dense than warm air, which makes it heavier. In this experiment the ice chills the air around the bag, then the cold air sinks to the bottom of the oatmeal box. That is why the temperature is lower when you check the thermometer the second time.

Something Extra

Here's a way to show that cold water sinks, too. Make an ice cube by freezing water mixed with food coloring. Put the ice cube in a glass of room-temperature water. As the ice melts, the cold, colored water will sink to the bottom of the glass to form a distinct layer.

Currents of Color

Which is heavier, warm water or cold water? This experiment in density will help you find the answer.

Materials

- paper cup
- pencil
- glass quart jar
- warm water
- measuring cup
- cold water
- ice
- food coloring

Directions

❶ Fill the glass jar nearly to the top with warm water.

❷ Use the pencil to poke four holes around the bottom edge of the cup.

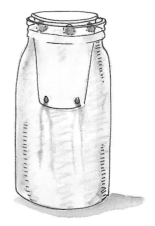

❸ Fill the measuring cup with $\frac{1}{2}$ cup of cold water. Stir in 5 drops of food coloring. Add two cubes of ice and stir.

❹ Place the paper cup into the warm water in the jar. Quickly pour the cold water into the cup. What happens when the cold, colored water contacts the warm water?

Action, Reaction, Results

Density is the measure of the amount of matter that is in a given space. The molecules of the cold water are more numerous and closer to each other than the molecules in a similar amount of warm water, so cold water is heavier. It sinks to the bottom of the jar in colorful curls.

Sink or Float

Salt water is heavier than fresh (plain, unsalted) water. An egg can help you to prove it.

Materials

- 2 glasses
- 5 tablespoons salt
- 2 raw eggs
- water

Directions

❶ Fill the first glass halfway with water. Mix in 5 tablespoons of salt. Gently place an egg on the salt water. Does it float or sink?

❷ Fill the second glass halfway with fresh water. Place an egg in the water. Does it float or sink?

Action, Reaction, Results

Salt water is more dense than fresh water because of the salt content. There is more matter in a given amount of salt water than there is in a similar amount of fresh water. The egg easily floats in the salt water, but not in the fresh water, because the egg is less dense than the salt water and more dense than the fresh water.

Oldie Moldy

Some plants reproduce by seeds and some reproduce by spores. The spores needed to grow your own mold are as close by as a patch of house dust.

Materials

- 3 pieces of bread
- spray bottle of water
- 3 self-sealing plastic sandwich bags
- stick-on labels
- marker

Directions

❶ Mist three slices of bread with water until they are damp but not soaking wet.

❷ Find a dusty spot— under a bed or in a closet—and wipe up some dust onto the bread. Slip the slice into a plastic bag and seal it. Label the bag and write down where you found the dust.

❸ Repeat the steps with the second piece of bread, but get dust from a different spot. Do the same with the third slice.

❹ Place all of the labeled bags in a warm, dark place. Check them daily but don't open the bags. On the fourth day, how does the bread look?

Action, Reaction, Results

Tiny spores float through the air and spread over great distances. Most house dust contains mold spores. When the spores finally come in contact with a moist place where food is available, they grow. The bread picks up mold spores when you rub it in house dust. The damp bread provides an excellent environment for the molds to reproduce and grow.

WORD FILE

- **Fungi:** Plural of fungus.
- **Mold:** A kind of fungus.
- **Spore:** A reproductive cell formed by certain plants such as ferns or fungi. The spores of fungi are often very tiny.

Baked Ice Cream

Insulation can keep things hot or cold. You can demonstrate how it works by baking a great ice cream treat in the oven.

Materials

- oven
- 2 egg whites
- 2 tablespoons sugar
- medium-sized glass bowl
- mixer
- 6 vanilla wafers
- cookie sheet
- spoon
- vanilla ice cream

Directions

❶ Preheat the oven to 250 degrees Fahrenheit.

❷ In a clean, dry glass bowl, whip two egg whites with the mixer on high. Beat 2 minutes. Add 2 tablespoons sugar. Whip until the mixture makes stiff, glossy peaks.

❸ Place the cookies on a cookie sheet. Spoon a walnut-sized mound of ice cream onto the center of each cookie.

❹ Coat each ice cream topped cookie with a thick layer of egg white mixture. Be sure to completely cover the ice cream and cookie. Bake them in the oven until the egg white turns light brown, about 3 or 4 minutes. Remove from the oven and enjoy. Is the ice cream still cold?

Action, Reaction, Results

Insulation prevents cold or heat from draining away. Layers of air within or between materials improve the efficiency of insulation. By whipping the egg whites you add air to the mixture. In the oven, the air bubbles prevent the heat from getting to the ice cream. When you eat the treat, the egg white mixture is warm, but the ice cream remains cold.

Something Extra
A similar dessert made with cake, ice cream, and egg whites is called a "Baked Alaska."

Water Bag

Punch a hole in a bag full of water, and you'll get all wet— unless the bag happens to be made from certain polymers.

Materials

- self-sealing plastic sandwich bag
- water
- sharp pencil

Directions

❶ Fill the plastic bag with water and seal it.

❷ Hold up the bag with one hand. Hold the pencil with the other hand, and in a quick, stabbing motion, stick it through one side of the bag and out the other. Does the bag leak?

Action, Reaction, Results

Certain types of molecules form long chains called polymers. Some are natural and some are manufactured. Polyethylene is a type of plastic made from polymers and used to make plastic bags. Polyethylene has a unique quality: it shrinks when ripped or when a hole is poked in it. When you poke a hole in the bag with the pencil, the plastic seals around the pencil and doesn't leak.

Down the Spout

Amaze your friends by pouring water from a pitcher into a glass two feet away.

Materials

- 1-quart pitcher
- water
- food coloring
- 3 feet of cloth string
- drinking glass

Directions

❶ Fill the pitcher halfway with water, add several drops of food coloring, and stir.

❷ Soak the string for a moment in the water, then take it out and let it drain back into the pitcher.

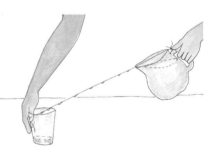

❸ Tie one end of the string to the handle of the pitcher. Set the glass on a flat surface 2 feet away.

❹ With one hand, hold the pitcher about a foot high. With the other hand, hold the loose end of the wet string. Stretch the string tightly across the spout of the pitcher, and hold the loose end against the inside of the glass.

❺ Slowly pour a trickle of colored water down the string and into the glass. Can you fill the glass without spilling?

Action, Reaction, Results

Cohesion is the tendency of a material to stick to itself. As you pour the water from the pitcher, it is attracted to the water on the already wet string. Another force is at work here as well. The molecules of some substances are attracted to the molecules of other substances. This is called adhesion. In this experiment, the water is attracted to the string and tends to cling to it.

Slip and Slide

If it weren't for friction, it would be difficult to stay on your feet as you walk across the floor. Use this demonstration to learn more about this gripping force.

Materials

- 2 blocks of wood about 3 inches square
- soap
- 2 flat metal jar lids
- cooking oil

Directions

❶ Quickly rub the 2 blocks of wood together for about a minute. Feel the inner surfaces of the wood blocks. Are they warm?

❷ Coat the inner surfaces of the wood blocks with a layer of soap. Rub them together again for about a minute, then check. Are they warm? Were they easier to rub together this time?

❸ Rub the flat surfaces of the two metal lids together for about a minute. Do they become warm? Do they make a noise?

❹ Coat the flat surfaces of the lids with cooking oil, then rub them together again. Do they feel warm this time? Did they make as much noise as they rubbed together?

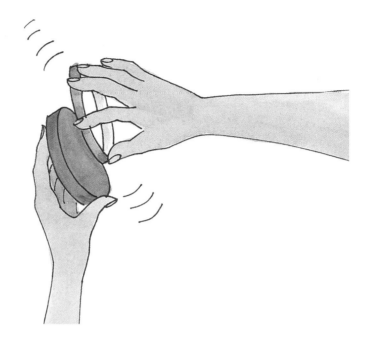

Action, Reaction, Results

Most surfaces are rough. Even those that look smooth have tiny imperfections. When two surfaces are rubbed together, the imperfections catch on each other and create resistance, or friction. It takes energy to make the surfaces move across each other, and much of that energy is turned into heat. The soap and oil are lubricants. They coat the surfaces and make them slide past each other more easily. With less friction, less heat is generated.

WORD FILE

- **Friction:** Force that offers resistance to movement between two or more surfaces.
- **Lubricant:** A slippery substance used to coat the surfaces of moving objects so that they move more easily past each other.

Something Extra

Friction can be put to good use. The brake on a bicycle works by friction. When it's used, the brake presses against the turning wheel and creates friction that slows or stops the wheel. Lubricants are useful, too. They are used to coat moving parts in machines to prevent them from wearing out or getting too hot.

Sweet or Salty

Sugar and salt certainly have different tastes, but they look a lot alike. Here's a way to tell them apart without tasting them.

Materials

- 2 small saucepans
- 1 teaspoon salt
- 1 teaspoon sugar
- stove

Directions

❶ Mix up the teaspoons so you are not sure which is salt and which is sugar.

❷ With an adult helper, place each saucepan on a burner on the stove. Put the contents of the first spoon in the first pan and the contents of the second spoon in the second pan.

❸ Turn on both burners to medium heat and watch for a few minutes. Do any changes take place?

Action, Reaction, Results

Nothing happens to the salt. It remains white and grainy. The sugar turns brown and begins to melt. Heating sugar causes its molecules to separate into carbon, turning it brown, and hydrogen and oxygen in the form of water.

WORD FILE

- **Carbon:** An element, which is a substance made up entirely of atoms of all the same kind.

Molecules on the Move

Take a close look at a glass of water. Can you see the water moving? You can't always believe your eyes because even though the water looks still, it is in motion.

Materials

- pint jar
- water
- food coloring

Directions

❶ Fill the pint jar to the top with cool tap water. Place the jar on a flat surface where it will not be disturbed.

❷ Tap several drops of food coloring into the water. Don't stir it. What does the food coloring do?

❸ Check the jar after 20 minutes. How does the food coloring look now?

Action, Reaction, Results

The water molecules in the jar are always on the move. They are so tiny that you can't see them move, but you can see the effect they have on the food coloring. As the streams of color settle, the particles of food coloring are hit by water molecules sending them in all different directions. Within an hour the color is evenly spread just by the moving molecules.

WORD FILE

- **Diffusion:** The spreading of molecules of a substance through another substance.
- **Particle:** A tiny part of a substance, such as a grain of sand or a molecule.

Making Mayonnaise

Mayonnaise looks simple on a sandwich, but to make this special spread, you have to make oil and "water" mix.

Materials

- blender
- 1 cup tofu
- 3 tablespoons vinegar
- $\frac{1}{2}$ cup olive oil
- glass pint jar with lid

Directions

❶ In the blender at slow speed, combine tofu and 1 tablespoon of vinegar.

❷ Adjust blender to medium and add olive oil very slowly, a drop at a time. Use about a third of the oil, then add a tablespoon of vinegar.

❸ Continue to add oil very slowly until two thirds has been added, then add the final tablespoon of vinegar. Blend in the last of the oil.

❹ Pour your mayonnaise into a jar and refrigerate. You might want to add a little salt before you use your mayonnaise on a sandwich.

Action, Reaction, Results

Mayonnaise is a substance known as an emulsion. Usually oil and water (in this case, oil and vinegar) don't mix. In this experiment, you use an emulsifier, the tofu, to surround the droplets of oil and separate them from each other. The individual oil droplets are suspended in the vinegar.

WORD FILE

- **Emulsifier:** A substance which surrounds liquid droplets and prevents them from touching each other.
- **Emulsion:** A substance in which drops of oil are suspended in another substance.

Fast Fall

Gravity is a force, or type of energy, that pulls all objects toward Earth. It holds people on the ground and keeps the Moon from flying off into space. If you pick up an object then let go of it, it falls down because of gravity.

Materials

- book
- rubber ball
- spoon
- pencil
- marble
- ball of crumpled aluminum foil

Directions

❶ Hold the book in one hand and the rubber ball in the other hand.

❷ Put your arms straight out in front of you. Make sure the book and the ball are the same distance from the floor.

❸ Let go of the book and the ball at exactly the same time. Watch them drop. Do they hit the floor at the same time?

Experiments You Can Do in Your Kitchen

❹ Repeat the experiment several times. Use a different pair of objects each time: a ball and a spoon, a pencil and a marble, a book and a ball of crumpled aluminum foil, and so on. Do the objects always hit the floor at the same time?

Action, Reaction, Results

The objects you dropped—the book, ball, spoon, pencil, marble, and ball of crumpled aluminum foil— were pulled down by gravity. The force of gravity on all these objects is equal, no matter how big or heavy they are. Therefore, all the objects fall at the same speed. In each part of this experiment, the pair of items you dropped fell at the same speed and hit the floor together.

Something Extra

Try the experiment with a pencil and a flat piece of paper. Now crumple up the paper and try it again. Do the two objects hit the floor at the same time in both cases? Why or why not?

A Matter of Balance

Even when you are sitting still, your muscles are constantly making tiny adjustments to keep you balanced. At the center of this balancing act is your center of gravity.

Materials

- 1-inch-thick slice of raw potato
- pencil
- corked bottle
- 2 forks

Directions

❶ Place the corked bottle on a flat surface.

❷ Try to balance the pencil on its point on the cork. Is it possible?

❸ Push the pencil through the center of the potato slice.

❹ Push the tines of the forks into the edge of the potato opposite each other.

❺ Now try to balance the pencil on its point on the cork. If it doesn't balance, adjust the forks until it does.

Action, Reaction, Results

All objects have a point of balance at which they are perfectly balanced and will not fall. This is called the center of gravity. At first, the pencil in this experiment cannot balance on its point. By adding the potato slice and forks you can adjust the setup until you find the proper center of gravity.

Soak It Up

Oh, no! The milk has spilled! What can you grab to soak up the mess? This experiment in absorption can help you find the answer.

Materials

- four clear plastic cups of equal size
- marker or pen
- water
- four 3-inch squares of different fabric (such as cotton, wool, nylon, rayon, polyester, or silk)

Directions

❶ Measure 2 inches up from the bottom of each cup and draw a line.

❷ Fill each cup with water to the line you drew. Place a square of fabric in each cup and press it down until it is completely wet.

❸ Remove each piece of fabric, one at a time. When you take the fabric out, hold it over the cup until it stops dripping, then set it down beside the cup. Do not squeeze the water out into the cup—just let it drip naturally.

❹ Mark the new water level on each cup, then measure the water level of each. Which cup has the least amount of water in it?

Action, Reaction, Results

Absorption is the taking up of a gas by a solid or liquid, or the taking up of a liquid by a solid. There are different ways that materials can be absorbed by other materials, but in the case of the fabrics in this experiment, it is capillary action at work. The fabrics are made up of tiny fibers. Water molecules move into the spaces between the fibers and are held within the fabric. As the water molecules move in, they attract other water molecules and draw them in, too. Fabrics with more fibers attract and hold fluids more easily than other fabrics.

Secret Message

You can surprise your friends by using this recipe for invisible ink.

Materials

- 1 lemon
- juicer
- small bowl
- cotton swab
- white paper
- lamp

Directions

❶ Squeeze the juice from the lemon into a small bowl.

❷ Dip the cotton swab into the lemon juice and use it to write an invisible message on a clean sheet of white paper. Allow the "ink" to dry.

❸ Hold the paper very close to—but not touching—an exposed light bulb. Move the paper so that the entire message is exposed to the heat from the bulb. What happens?

Action, Reaction, Results

The lemon juice contains carbon compounds. When exposed to heat, these compounds tend to turn brown or black. When heated with the light bulb, the invisible message turns dark and becomes readable.

WORD FILE

- **Compound:** A substance that contains two or more elements.

Cling, Cling, Cling

Have you ever had an article of clothing get all "clingy" on you? That's static electricity at work.

Materials

- 1 cup dry puffed rice cereal
- small glass bowl
- plastic wrap
- adhesive tape
- metal spoon

Directions

❶ Lightly crush the cereal in your hand and let it fall into the bowl.

❷ Cover the top of the bowl with a piece of plastic wrap and tape it in place so that the surface is smooth and tight.

❸ Make a fist and rub your knuckles back and forth across the wrap for about 30 seconds, or until the cereal begins to cling to the underside of the wrap.

❹ Once the plastic wrap
is covered with cereal,
rub the bowl of the
metal spoon gently
across the surface
of the plastic wrap.
The cereal will drop
off again.

Action, Reaction, Results

Atoms are made up of very tiny particles. Some of the particles (protons and electrons) have a property called charge. Protons have a positive charge, and electrons have a negative charge. Charges that are the same push each other away, and charges that are different attract each other. Static electricity is a buildup of charge on the surface of an object. By rubbing the plastic wrap, you build up static electricity that attracts the cereal. The metal spoon neutralizes the static electricity, and the cereal is no longer attracted to the wrap.

Something Extra

For more fun with static electricity, use a hole puncher to punch out some circles from a piece of plain white paper. Rub a wool scarf across a hard rubber or plastic comb, then pass the comb over the paper circles without touching them. What happens? Leave the comb undisturbed overnight, then check it in the morning. Does it still attract the paper?

Lightning Strikes

Have you ever walked across a carpet, then gotten a shock when you touched something? That's static electricity at work.

Materials

- large plastic bag
- lightweight tin baking sheet
- small metal object, such as a key
- wood table
- baseball-sized piece of clay

Directions

❶ Place the plastic bag, baking sheet, and metal object on a wood tabletop.

❷ Press the clay into the center of the sheet so that it sticks to it. Grasp the clay and rub the bottom of the sheet back and forth on top of the plastic bag for a minute or two. Do not touch any part of the sheet while you are doing this.

❸ Turn off all the lights in the room to make it easier to see the spark. Using the clay as a handle, pick up the sheet and hold it near the metal object on the table. A small spark should jump from the sheet to the metal object.

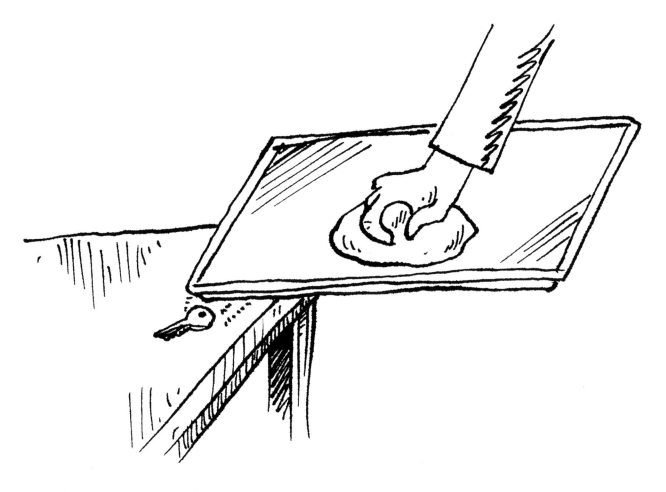

Action, Reaction, Results

Static electricity is a buildup of charge on the surface of an object. By rubbing the plastic bag, you cause static electricity to build up on the baking sheet. The wooden table and the clay do not attract static electricity, but the key does. Because the key and the tray have unlike charges, the static electricity on the tray jumps to the key. You see this transfer as a spark.

Something Extra

For more fun with static electricity, cut out 10 small paper butterflies. Rub a wool scarf across a hard rubber comb, then pass the comb over the butterflies without touching them. Watch the butterflies flutter. How long does the static electricity have an effect on the butterflies?

Rockets Away!

Three hundred years ago Sir Isaac Newton figured out how and why things move. Get set to blast off with one of Newton's Laws of Motion.

Materials

- 11 feet of plastic fishing line
- plastic drinking straw
- oblong-shaped balloon
- paper clip
- tape

Directions

❶ Slip one end of the fishing line through the drinking straw. Find a place where you can stretch the fishing line at least 10 feet and tie each end to something secure. Attach both ends of the line, making sure that the line is taut.

❷ Blow up the balloon and secure the end with the paper clip.

❸ Tape the balloon rocket to the straw as shown.

❹ Position the balloon at the beginning of the line. Remove the paper clip to release the rocket.

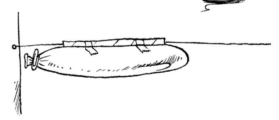

Action, Reaction, Results

Newton's Third Law of Motion states that every action has an equal and opposite reaction. When you remove the paper clip, the air escapes from the balloon in one direction. This action produces a reaction: The balloon moves forward in the opposite direction.

Special Spoons

Have you ever held a cup of hot cocoa on a cold day and felt your hands getting warmer? That feeling is the result of heat conduction.

Materials

- butter, slightly softened
- three spoons, roughly the same size (one metal, one wood, one plastic)
- three small beads
- cup, filled with hot water

Directions

❶ Place a pea-sized dab of butter at the end of each spoon handle.

❷ Push a bead into each dab of butter.

❸ Place the spoons into the cup of hot water with the handles pointing up. Make sure that the handles do not touch each other. Which bead falls first?

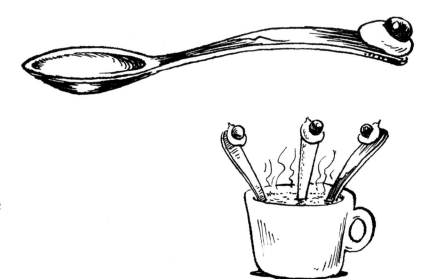

Action, Reaction, Results

When something is heated, its molecules begin to move faster. Moving molecules bump into other molecules, making them move, too. This process, called conduction, is one way heat energy spreads. Some materials are better conductors than others. For instance, metal is a good conductor. When you do this experiment, the heat from the water tends to move more quickly up the metal spoon, warming the butter and causing that bead to fall first.

Temperature Trouble

To find out if something is hot or cold, you can measure its temperature with a thermometer. You can also feel it with your hand.

Materials

- three large bowls
- water
- ice cubes
- flat surface

Directions

❶ Fill the first bowl with water and ice cubes, so that the water is very cold.

❷ Fill the second bowl with lukewarm water.

❸ Ask an adult to help you fill the third bowl with hot tap water. HAVE AN ADULT MAKE SURE IT'S NOT HOT ENOUGH TO HURT YOU.

❹ Line the bowls up on a flat surface, with the hot water on the left side, the lukewarm water in the center, and the ice water on the right side.

❺ Place your left hand into the hot water and your right hand into the ice water. Slowly count to 30 while you keep your hands in the water.

❻ Now quickly remove your hands from the hot and cold water, and place both hands in the lukewarm water. Does one of your hands feel cool? Does one of your hands feel warm? If so, which one feels cool and which one feels warm?

Action, Reaction, Results

When you put your hands in the lukewarm water, your hands did not really feel the temperature of the water. They felt the difference in temperature between the lukewarm water and the water they had been in. When your left hand was in hot water, it felt hot. The lukewarm water was cooler, so it made your left hand feel cool. When your right hand was in cold water, it felt cold. The lukewarm water was warmer, so it made your right hand feel warm. This experiment shows that your hands can't always judge the temperature of water.

Something Extra

Prepare two bowls of icy cold water. Put a glove on one hand, and leave the other hand bare. Place a plastic bag over each hand. Ask an adult to fasten the bags at your wrists with loose rubber bands. Put each hand into a bowl of icy water. Be sure to keep the tops of the bags out of the water. Which hand feels warm longer? Why?

Float and Sink

Some objects float on water and other objects sink in water. An object's density is how much it weighs compared to its volume, or how much space it takes up. Objects that are less dense than water (weigh less than water in the same amount of space) float. Objects that are more dense than water (weigh more than water in the same amount of space) sink.

Materials

- clay
- large bowl
- water
- flat surface

Directions

❶ Divide your clay into two equal parts.

❷ Roll one half of the clay into a ball.

❸ Shape the other half of the clay into a flat-bottomed boat.

❹ Put water into the bowl and place it on a flat surface.

❺ Place the clay ball into the water. Does it sink or float? Why?

❻ Now take out the clay ball, and put the clay boat into the water. Does it sink or float? Why?

Action, Reaction, Results

In this experiment, the clay ball and the clay boat weigh about the same. The clay ball, however, has less volume, or takes up less space, than the clay boat. In other words, the ball is more dense than the boat. The ball sinks because it is more dense than water. The boat floats because it is less dense than water.

Something Extra
Gather several different objects, such as a rock, apple, piece of paper, small plastic bowl, spoon, penny, leaf, and so on. Guess which objects will float and which will sink. Then place each object in a bowl of water and see if you guessed correctly.

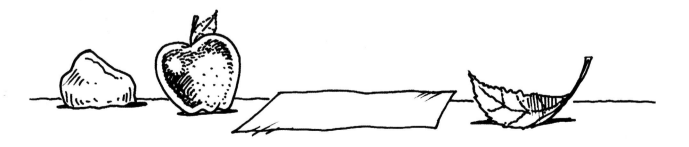

All Dried Up

You'll need 2 weeks to complete this experiment to see how desiccation can be used for preservation.

Materials

- $\frac{1}{2}$ cup baking soda
- $\frac{1}{2}$ cup salt
- plastic cup
- knife
- two small potatoes
- plastic wrap
- adhesive tape

Directions

❶ Pour the baking soda and salt into a plastic cup. Cover the opening of the cup with your hand and shake the contents to mix them thoroughly.

❷ Ask your adult helper to cut a 1-inch-thick slice from the center of a potato. Poke it down into the middle of the mixture. Cover the cup with plastic wrap and seal it with adhesive tape. Place the cup in a cool, dry spot for 1 week.

❸ At the end of the week, remove the potato slice from the mixture. Next, have your helper cut a 1-inch-thick slice from the center of another potato. Place both the fresh and dried slices of potato on a clean, dry surface that is exposed to air for 5 days.

❹ At the end of 5 days, check the potato slices. Do they show signs of decay? Which one is better preserved?

Action, Reaction, Results

Decay is the result of the work of tiny microorganisms called bacteria. Bacteria need water to survive. The salt in the first part of the experiment draws the water from the potato slice—this is called desiccation. The dried potato is more resistant to decay and survives, while the untreated potato begins to rot.

Two or Three

Tearing a piece of writing paper into three equal parts is easy. That is, unless the force applied is unequal.

Materials

- 9- by 9-inch piece of writing paper
- pencil
- scissors

Directions

❶ Fold the paper in half, top to bottom, then unfold and lay it flat. Place a ruler horizontally along the fold and make a pencil mark on the paper at the 3-inch point and the 6-inch point.

❷ Draw two vertical lines from each pencil mark to the top edge of the paper. Cut along the lines using the scissors.

❸ Pick up the cut side of the paper by the two outside corners and hold it in front of you. Pulling on the corners, try to rip the paper into three equal pieces.

Action, Reaction, Results

Force is what causes something to change what it is doing. Mechanics is the study of interactions between matter and the forces acting on it. In this experiment, with all other factors being equal, the amount of mechanical force applied to both sides of the paper has to be exactly the same in order to tear it into three equal parts. When you try to rip the paper into three equal parts, no matter how hard you try, the amount of force you apply is unequal and the paper tears into two pieces. If you are right-handed, it is usually the piece on the right that tears away.

Slip and Slide

What force helps to keep a book from sliding off a table? Friction helps keep things in their place.

Materials

- thumbtack
- wide rubber band
- 3-inch-long block of 2- by 4-inch wood
- pencil and paper
- a variety of surfaces (for example, wood, a carpet sample, sandpaper, tile, or glass)

Directions

❶ Use a thumbtack to attach the rubber band to one end of the wood block.

❷ Place the wood block on a flat surface. Measure the length of the unstretched rubber band and record it.

❸ Pull gently on the rubber band until the block begins to slide. Measure the length of the stretched rubber band at that point and record it.

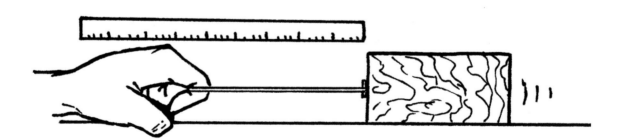

❹ Repeat step 3 on the different surfaces and record the results. Does the block slide more easily on rough or on smooth surfaces? Does the length of the rubber band change depending on the surface?

Action, Reaction, Results

Friction is the resistance that one surface has when moving over another surface that it comes in contact with. It takes force to overcome the force of friction. In this experiment, you supply the force needed by pulling on the rubber band. Still, the resistance is not easy to overcome. The rougher the surface, the harder it is to get the block to move. Instead of moving the object, the applied force stretches the rubber band. The greater the friction between the wooden block and the surface, the more force must be applied, and the longer the band becomes before the object finally moves.

Something Extra
A lubricant is something that reduces friction between two surfaces. Oil is a lubricant. Try rubbing some on the wood block, then measure how much force it takes to move it. Is it easier? Are there other lubricants you can test? What about soap? What do these lubricants have in common?

Going Up

Oxygen can be found all around us—in air, in water, and as part of this experiment in oxidation.

Materials

- untreated steel wool pad that does not contain soap
- water glass
- water
- shallow glass bowl

Directions

❶ Stuff the steel wool pad securely into the bottom of the glass so that it will not fall out. Add water to moisten the pad, then pour out the water.

❷ Pour about 1 inch of water into the shallow bowl. Turn the glass over and set it rim-side down in the bowl.

❸ Observe the water level in the glass every hour for at least 8 hours. Does it change?

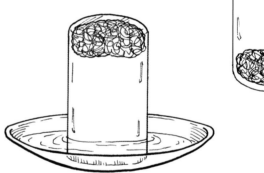

Action, Reaction, Results

Over time, the water level in the glass rises. At first, the glass is filled with air that keeps the water out. After a while, the wet steel wool begins to rust. Rust that is produced as iron in the steel wool combines with oxygen in the air—an example of a process called oxidation. Slowly, the oxygen in the glass is used up, lowering the air pressure inside it. The higher air pressure outside the glass pushes down on the water in the bowl, causing the level in the glass to rise. About one-fifth of the air in the glass is made up of oxygen. Once that is used up, the process stops.